With lots of love,
Luke Puffer
Grandma and Grandpa Brown

Reading Opens Our World

WHEN DINOSAURS LIVED

Stegosaurus

KATE RIGGS

Published by
CREATIVE EDUCATION

P.O. Box 227, Mankato, Minnesota 56002
Creative Education is an imprint of The Creative Company
www.thecreativecompany.us

Design and production by Danny Nanos of Gilbert & Nanos
Art direction by Rita Marshall
Printed by Corporate Graphics in the United States of America

Photographs by Alamy (Martin Bache), American Museum of Natural History
(Denis Finnin), Bridgeman Art Library (English Photographer, English School,
Arthur Oxenham, Roger Payne), Corbis (Paul A. Souders), Getty Images
(DEA Picture Library, Ken Lucas), Library of Congress

Library of Congress Cataloging-in-Publication Data
Riggs, Kate.
Stegosaurus / by Kate Riggs.
p. cm.
Summary: A brief introduction to the armored *Stegosaurus*,
highlighting its size, habitat, food sources, and demise. Also included is a
virtual field trip to a museum with notable *Stegosaurus* fossils.

Includes bibliographical references and index.

ISBN 978-1-60818-118-6

1. Stegosaurus—Juvenile literature. I. Title.

QE862.O65R556 2012

567.915'3—dc22   2010049332

CPSIA: 030111 PO1451

FIRST EDITION

2 4 6 8 9 7 5 3 1

CREATIVE EDUCATION

Table of Contents

Stegosaurus was a stegosaur dinosaur. It lived from 154 to 144 million years ago. The name *Stegosaurus* means "roof lizard."

Stegosaurus might have had green skin that looked like a lizard's

SOUND IT OUT

Stegosaurus: *STEG-oh-SORE-us*

Stegosaurus had 2 rows of 17 bony plates that stuck up along its back and tail. It had four spikes at the end of its tail, too. *Stegosaurus* had a small head with a tiny brain.

Scientists first thought the plates lay flat or were lined up evenly

An adult *Stegosaurus* was as tall as an elephant—about 14 feet (4.3 m). It weighed 3.4 tons (3 t) and grew to be about 30 feet (9 m) long. *Stegosaurus* moved slowly on its four thick legs. Some people think that it could have stood up on its back legs.

Stegosaurus's back legs were twice as long as its front legs

Stegosaurus lived in the warm forests and plains of North America. It had relatives in other parts of the world, too. Some kinds of stegosaurs lived in Europe, Africa, and Asia.

Stegosaurus lived during a time called the Jurassic

SOUND IT OUT

Europe: *YOO-rup*

Stegosaurus was a plant-eater. Its neighbors were other plant-eaters such as the long-necked *Apatosaurus* and *Diplodocus*. The meat-eating *Allosaurus* was a dangerous predator of *Stegosaurus*. *Stegosaurus* defended itself with its body armor.

Stegosaurs in Europe were also hunted by giant meat-eaters

Stegosaurs ate food all day long. Ferns, cycads, and bushy evergreen plants called conifers were their favorites. *Stegosaurus* died out about 144 million years ago. By 99 million years ago, all the stegosaurs had disappeared. Then, all the dinosaurs died out 65 million years ago.

Stegosaurus used its beak, or mouth, to grab plants

Scientists know about *Stegosaurus* because they have studied fossils. Fossils are the remains of living things that died long ago. Many fossils of *Stegosaurus* have been found in Colorado and other places in the western United States. The first one was found in 1877.

Some kinds of rock, like sandstone, are good places to find fossils

Stegosaurus compared
with a five-foot-tall
(152 cm) person

Paleontologists are people who study dinosaurs. Othniel C. Marsh was the paleontologist who named *Stegosaurus*. He called it "roof lizard" because he thought that the plates on *Stegosaurus*'s back lay flat, like shingles on a roof.

For a while, people thought that *Stegosaurus*'s plates were lined up in one row. Now scientists know that they were in two, uneven rows. But scientists still study *Stegosaurus*. There are more things to learn about this "roof lizard"!

Museums show what people think
Stegosaurus looked like

A Virtual Field Trip: American Museum of Natural History, New York, New York

You can see *Stegosaurus* skeletons at the American Museum of Natural History in New York, New York. There are more dinosaur fossils at this museum than at any other museum in the world! The American Museum also has a cast, or model, of the first young *Stegosaurus* ever found. The small cast stands next to a skeleton of an adult *Stegosaurus*.

Glossary

armor—protective coverings, such as plates or spikes

cycads—plants that look like palm trees and have big cones, or dry fruit

evergreen—green all the time; evergreen plants have leaves that stay green year round

predators—animals that kill and eat other animals

stegosaur—a small-headed, plant-eating dinosaur that had four legs and a double row of bony plates along its back and tail

Stegosaurus at the American
Museum of Natural History

Read More

Dixon, Dougal. *Plant-eating Dinosaurs*. Mankato, Minn.: NewForest Press, 2011.

Johnson, Jinny. *Triceratops and Other Horned and Armored Dinosaurs*. North Mankato, Minn.: Smart Apple Media, 2008.

Web Sites

Dinosaur Facts

http://www.thelearningpage.org/dinosaurs/dinosaur_facts.htm
This site has a fact sheet about *Stegosaurus* that can be printed out.

Enchanted Learning: Stegosaurus

http://www.enchantedlearning.com/subjects/dinosaurs/facts/Stegosaurus
This site has *Stegosaurus* facts and a picture to color.

Index